A Walk Thru the Book of

JOHN

A Surprising Savior

Walk Thru the Bible

BakerBooks

a division of Baker Publishing Group
Grand Rapids, Michigan

Published by Baker Books
a division of Baker Publishing Group
P.O. Box 6287, Grand Rapids, MI 49516-6287
www.bakerbooks.com

Printed in the United States of America

Library of Congress Cataloging-in-Publication Data
A walk thru the book of John : a surprising savior / Walk Thru the Bible.
    p. cm.
   Includes bibliographical references.
   ISBN 978-0-8010-7173-7 (pbk.)
    1. Bible. N.T. John—Study and teaching. 2. Bible. N.T. John—Criticism, inter-
pretation, etc. I. Walk Thru the Bible (Educational ministry).
   BS2616.W28 2009
   226.50071—dc22   2008050826

Cover image: naphtalina / iStock

Contents

Introduction   5

Session 1   A Tent of His Presence   11
Session 2   A Surprising Savior   20
Session 3   Jesus on Trial—Again   29
Session 4   Light in Darkness   37
Session 5   Lord of Life   45
Session 6   Secrets of the Heart   53
Session 7   Clash of Kingdoms   60
Session 8   Hope Lives   67

Conclusion   75
Leader's Notes   76
Bibliography   78

Introduction

The planet lay shrouded in darkness, lifeless and empty, and devoid of any hint of purpose. But at a word, a Spirit moved over the surface, brooding and breathing over the deep waters, and light and life began to take form. This dramatic genesis reached its fulfillment when the Creator breathed his Spirit into a mound of dust and called it human. The dust came to life, and the earth was filled with purpose and passion and a plan. This life was made in the image of God.

Things did not go well. The humans squandered their gift, and the image was shattered. Another kind of darkness shrouded the planet, relentlessly aiming to return it to its dark and lifeless nature. But the Creator intervened. He prophesied of another genesis. And thousands of years later, a light entered the darkness and a new creation was born.

That's the cosmic picture behind the gospel of John. It's the story of a re-genesis, a new birth, a light piercing the darkness and restoring life to an entombed vestige of the image of God. That light, of course, is Jesus. His truth penetrates lies, and his life brings the dead out of the grave. He is the beginning of the new creation.

John's gospel is different than the other three biblical records of Jesus's life and ministry. It evokes more big-picture images and paints more details into certain aspects of the Savior's work than do Matthew, Mark, and Luke. Likely written later than the other gospels, it fills in some of the gaps and explores some of Jesus's teachings at a deeper level. It adds texture and depth to the disruptive nature of the light that came into the darkness and exposed its lies. And it explores more fully the mysterious bond between Father, Son, Spirit, and those who believe.

Themes

Several recurring themes in John give it a unique flavor among the gospels:

Where Jesus has come from and where he is going. The gospel begins with a startling statement of Jesus's identity: he is the Word that became flesh. Not only was he *with* God, but he *was* God. After the prologue in the first few verses, the gospel is a progressive unveiling of Jesus as God incarnate. One way John highlights the tension in his audience's perception of Jesus's humanity and his divinity is to repeatedly raise the question of where Jesus came from and where he is going. For example, Jesus tells Nicodemus in 3:13 that "no one has ever gone into heaven except the one who came from heaven—the Son of Man." When Jesus identifies himself as the true bread that "came down" out of heaven, the crowd marvels: "Is this not Jesus, the son of Joseph, whose father and mother we know? How can he now say, 'I came down from heaven'?" (6:42).

He tells the religious authorities, "I know where I came from and where I am going. But you have no idea where I come from or where I am going" (8:14). And he informs his disciples, "I am going there to prepare a place for you. . . . I will come back and take you to be with me that you also may be where I am. You know the way to the place where I am going" (14:2–4). The reason this issue of coming and going shows up so frequently is to reinforce the truth that Jesus is no ordinary human. He is the light that is "coming into the world" (1:9).

Light and darkness. The interplay between light and darkness is pervasive in John's gospel. As early as 1:4, Jesus is identified as the light of men. Nicodemus comes to him in the darkness of night, and during their conversation, he points out that "light has come into the world, but men loved darkness instead of light because their deeds were evil" (3:19). Jesus calls himself the Light of the World (8:12; 9:5), and he tells his disciples that though they will only have the light a little while longer, they can become sons of light (12:35–36). In fact, this is Jesus's purpose: "I have come into the world as a light, so that no one who believes in me should stay in darkness" (12:46).

Glory. John says, "We have seen his glory" (1:14), and the revelation of glory becomes a progressive theme of the gospel. The first of Jesus's miracles revealed his glory (2:11), and glimpses of glory lead up to the cross and resurrection, which Jesus approaches with a focus on the glory it will bring. "Father, glorify your name!" he cries out the week before the crucifixion. "Then a voice came from heaven, 'I have glorified it, and will glorify it again'" (12:28). And his high-priestly prayer in chapter 17 is full of references to how Jesus glorifies the Father, how the Father glorifies him, and how he shares his glory with those who believe in him.

Seeing and believing. John 2–12 is often called "the book of signs," a collection of seven miracles that cultivate faith in many of the people who witness them and anger others. (See session 5 for a list of the seven signs.) Dialogue in the gospel often features those who believe because of what they've seen, those who don't believe in spite of what they've seen, and those who believe to a point but don't fully entrust themselves to Jesus's teaching. The climax of this theme is Jesus's statement to Thomas after the resurrection: "Because you have seen me, you have believed; blessed are those who have not seen and yet have believed" (20:29). This is followed by John's statement of purpose in writing: "Jesus did many other miraculous signs in the presence of his disciples, which are not recorded in this book. But these are written *that you may believe* that Jesus is the Christ, the Son of God, and that by believing you may have life in his name" (20:30–31; emphasis added).

Spirit, wind, and breath. There's only one word for these three meanings in both Hebrew (*ruach*) and Greek (*pneuma*). John takes full advantage of the triple meanings, especially in 3:8: "The *pneuma* blows wherever it pleases. You hear its sound, but you cannot tell where it comes from or where it is going. So it is with everyone born of the *pneuma*." After the resurrection, Jesus breathes on the disciples to give them the Spirit.

Spirit and flesh. The Holy Spirit plays a prominent role in John's gospel—the promise of his coming is clearer in chapters 14–16 than anywhere else in Scripture—and the Spirit is often specifically contrasted to the flesh. For example, "Flesh gives birth to flesh, but the Spirit gives birth to spirit" (3:6), and "The Spirit gives life; the flesh counts for nothing" (6:63). But most likely in order to combat early strains of Gnostic thought, John affirms the flesh as good. Gnosticism, when it fully developed in the second century, would emphasize the spiritual and consider the flesh evil, insisting that Jesus came in spirit but only appeared to have a body. It's in John's gospel that Jesus most clearly hungers, thirsts, gets tired, weeps, bleeds, and dies. The Holy Spirit will come to inhabit earthly flesh, not condemn it.

Wisdom incarnate. John uses imagery and terminology from Proverbs and extra-biblical wisdom literature to portray Jesus as wisdom incarnate. The wisdom that was with God at the foundation of the world is remarkably similar to the ministry of Jesus in John. Proverbs 8:22–36 is not only a good description of eternal wisdom, it's a good description of Jesus's ministry in this gospel.

Father and Son. The relationship between God the Father and Jesus the Son is emphasized, especially in Jesus's dialogue with religious authorities in chapter 8. Jesus's opponents remind him that their father is Abraham but also that God is their only Father—to which Jesus responds that they would love him if God was truly their Father, whereas in fact their real father is the devil. The Father's relationship to the Son is explored more fully in 1:14, 3:35, 5:17–23, 6:37–46, 10:14–18, 10:25–30, 14:6–12, and 16:25–28, among other passages. The clearest and boldest statement of the relationship between Father and Son is 10:30: "I and the Father are one."

How to Use This Guide

The questions in this guide are geared to elicit every participant's input, regardless of his or her level of preparation. Obviously, the more group members prepare by reading the biblical text and the background information in the study guide, the more they will get out of it. But even in busy weeks that afford no preparation time, everyone will be able to participate in a meaningful way.

The discussion questions also allow your group quite a bit of latitude. Some groups prefer to briefly discuss the questions in order to cover as many as possible, while others focus only on one or two of them in order to have more in-depth conversations. Since this study is designed for flexibility, feel free to adapt it according to the personality and needs of your group.

Each session ends with a hypothetical situation that relates to the passage of the week. Discussion questions are provided, but group members may also want to consider role-playing the scenario or setting up a two-team debate over one or two of the questions. These exercises often cultivate insights that wouldn't come out of a typical discussion.

Regardless of how you use this material, the biblical text will always be the ultimate authority. Your discussions may take you to many places and cover many issues, but they will have the greatest impact when they begin and end with God's Word itself. And never forget that the Spirit who inspired the Word is in on the discussion too. May he guide it—and you—wherever he wishes.

A Tent of His Presence

JOHN 1–3

Naqdimon hurried to the backstreet rendezvous, hoping no one would recognize him in the dark. He had asked for this covert meeting because he needed to know the truth, but his interest couldn't become public knowledge. Not yet. Not for someone in his position. No, tonight he was merely on a fact-finding mission; at least that would be his story if anyone spotted him. He would have to justify his reconnaissance as an unpleasant but necessary responsibility for a leader in charge of the nation's spiritual health. But deep down, his heart was more invested than that—hence, the secrecy. Tonight, the shadows would be his friends.

When he arrived at the designated place, his appointment was already standing there—with a couple of companions. Not ideal company, but no matter; considering the normal entourage, he'd settle for this more intimate gathering. Besides, this man's friends didn't run in Naqdimon's circles. The secret of this late-night venture would, most likely, be safe.

Naqdimon greeted his guests quickly and then got down to business. "Listen," he began. "We know you're genuine. You couldn't do the things you're doing if you weren't. We . . . well, *I* . . . just want to know what it all means. Are you . . . the One?"

Yeshua smiled. *The One*, he thought to himself. If only Naqdimon knew. Then, after a silence that lasted way too long for Naqdimon's comfort, he answered. "Honestly, my friend, this is the way it is. Unless a man . . . unless *you*, to be specific, are born from above, you will never be able to see the truth you're looking for."

Yeshua calmly watched Naqdimon's puzzled expression. "What do you mean? . . . how? . . ." Naqdimon knew that expression well—being "born anew"—but how did it apply to him? He was one of Israel's seventy, a member of the Sanhedrin. One of its wealthiest and most influential members, in fact. A sage, by all estimations. And he, of all people, was to be reborn like a convert to the faith?

"You're surprised?" Yeshua remarked. "You, a highly respected teacher, don't know this one elemental fact? It's true. You have to be born from above, from the Spirit. He's like the wind. It blows where it wishes, even though you can't see where it's coming from or where it's going. That's what finding the truth is like. The Spirit will show you what you did not expect to find—*if* you'll be born of him."

This rendition of John 3 captures the flavor, if not the exact details, of Nicodemus's encounter with Jesus. It was a quest for truth from someone who risked his entire reputation, and perhaps his career, to find God in closer, more real terms than he already knew. And Nicodemus's quest is ours too. We seek a real encounter with the living God. If we're hungry enough, we'll risk a lot to find him as he is.

Some aren't hungry enough, you know. Some people don't want the reality of Jesus to rearrange their world. Nicodemus surely felt that tension, which is why he went under the cover of night. But he went. He had to know.

The gospel of John begins with the answer to humanity's quest for God, and the rest of the book serves as courtroom testimony that the answer is true. The reader is taken on a remarkable journey to encounter a remarkable visitation from above—the God who clothed himself in flesh dwelled among us. And the story begins . . . well, before the world began.

The Word: John 1

Focus: John 1:1–18

"The LORD brought me forth as the first of his works, before his deeds of old; I was appointed from eternity, from the beginning, before the world began." So speaks the voice of wisdom in Proverbs 9:22–23. This voice is the *davar* of God, in Hebrew—or *logos* in the Greek translation of Scripture quoted by New Testament writers. It's the Word by which the Creator brought all things into existence, the Torah (law) upon which the world was founded.

Greek philosophers also spoke of a *logos*. For them, the term referred to the rational order, the natural law, the logic behind reality. In Greek thought, the world functioned on this im-

THE LIVING TABERNACLE

"Have them make a sanctuary for me, and I will dwell among them," God told Moses at Mount Sinai. "Make this tabernacle and all its furnishings exactly like the pattern I will show you" (Exod. 25:8–9). That pattern involved very specific dimensions, materials, and positioning, every detail of which was symbolic of God's relationship with and ministry on behalf of humanity. The tabernacle was made of earthly substances and was designed to be moved wherever God led the Israelites to go. It was fashioned after the true blueprints of God's presence in heaven (Heb. 8:5). It was where God reached out to his people.

When John writes that the Word became flesh and dwelled among us, he uses tabernacle words. Literally, Jesus "pitched his tent," or "tabernacled," among us. Like the tabernacle in the wilderness, the Messiah's body was made of earthly material, but it was where God's glory dwelled. Jesus was—and is—the living "tent of meeting" between God and humanity.

personal operating system. It too was the wisdom behind the cosmos.

The opening verses of John's gospel allude to Genesis 1:1—"in the beginning"—and blend Hebrew and Greek concepts of the *logos*. This mysterious wisdom preexisting the universe and governing it behind the scenes was with God and, in fact, *is* God. And, in a turn of events astonishing both in Hebrew and in Greek thought, this Word became flesh. Wisdom isn't formless after all, and the *logos* isn't impersonal. The Word is a knowable, eternal being who pursues a relationship with his people.

The prologue to John is the key to grasping the message of the rest of the book. In order to understand the works and words of Jesus, one has to understand where he came from and, as the gospel will make clear, where he is going. Always existing, he came down from heaven—God wrapping himself in human flesh. Because of his descent from and his eventual ascent to heaven, he is able to shine true light into the darkness, to give us the right to become children of God, and to make God known. He is the very essence of God in human form.

Discuss

- Though the world was made through Jesus, "the world did not recognize him" (1:10). Why do you think the world didn't recognize its own Creator? More specifically, why do you think the chosen people didn't recognize their Messiah?

  _____

  _____

  _____

  _____

- What do you think John means when he says, "we have seen his glory"?

  _____

  _____

  _____

  _____

The Wedding: John 2

Focus: John 2:1–11, 23–25

Jewish weddings lasted for days. As Jesus and his disciples celebrate in Cana with a bride and groom who are beginning their new life together, the wine runs out. Though this could be somewhat embarrassing to the couple's family, there are certainly

15

merchants around who would be glad to sell them some more wine to keep the festivities going. But the need never gets that far. Jesus's mother comes to him with the facts of the situation, and, in a response that sounds harsher in English than it was in Aramaic, he points out that the Father has a timetable that his mother doesn't know. Still, she knows who he is—she's been carrying the knowledge of his glory for roughly thirty years—and she believes he will act. And she's right. He does. He miraculously changes about 180 gallons of water into wine.

Jesus's first miracle in the gospel of John is at this wedding—an appropriate setting for the ultimate bridegroom who has come to receive his bride. It's an extravagant miracle that's rich with symbolism. The water, contained in six stone jars, was used for ritual purification. Jesus makes a major theological statement by transforming ritual water into new wine—a symbol of the messianic age. The abundance of the kingdom now fills the containers once reserved for the obligations of the law, and the result is joyful and life-giving—just like a wedding feast. It's the first of many ways that Jesus will reveal his glory, and it leads to faith (2:11).

For many, however, this is not a complete faith. At the end of chapter 2, Jesus receives the people's belief with a degree of mistrust. Why? Because he knows how easily hearts can turn.

Discuss

- John is the only gospel writer to tell the story of the wedding at Cana. Why do you think he felt it was important to include? What does it demonstrate about Jesus?

  _____

  _____

  _____

  _____

BORN AGAIN

The Talmud—a collection of rabbinic commentary on Jewish Scripture— speaks of proselytes as those who are "reborn." The conversion ritual for a Gentile involved an immersion into water and a literal "re-creation" as an Israelite. Legally, Gentiles reborn as Jews were new creatures whose prior family relationships no longer existed. Everything in his or her life became new.

Nicodemus would have been familiar with this terminology. His shock at Jesus's words about being born again were probably not from confusion about reentering a mother's womb. (His response to that effect may have been more of a rhetorical comment on the fact that, having been born as a Jew to a Jewish mother, it was impossible to convert to Judaism. "How can a Jew re-become a Jew?") Jesus reaffirms to him that ethnic or ritual Jewishness does not equal salvation. He—and all other Jews, as well as Gentiles—must be born of the Spirit in order to enter the kingdom.

The Wind: John 3

Focus: John 3:1–21

The conversation between Naqdimon and Yeshua—Nicodemus and Jesus—is one of the best-known passages of the New Testament. This Nicodemus may be the same enormously wealthy Nicodemus who later plays a role in the Jewish revolt of the late AD 60s, but whether or not that's true, we know from John that he becomes a secret follower of Jesus (see 7:50 and 19:39). At the time of this conversation, he's an influential member of the Sanhedrin—the Jewish court of seventy ruling elders (plus the high priest)—a Pharisee who is honestly seeking the truth and, unlike many of his colleagues, recognizes the evidence of God's hand on Jesus.

17

After Jesus's explanation that Nicodemus must be born again, or "from above," to see the kingdom of heaven, he gives the seeker a graphic picture of his role. In Numbers 21, God had judged some bitter, complaining Israelites by sending venomous snakes among them. The only way they could survive was to look at a bronze serpent God had instructed Moses to make and fix to the end of a pole. That serpent—a symbol of the curse—was lifted up for all to see. Those who would look to it lived. Those who wouldn't, didn't.

That, says Jesus, is a picture of his purpose. The Son of God himself becomes a symbol of the curse. He's lifted up on a stake, and those who look to him in faith will survive the judgment. And this is his desire; God loved the world so much that he sent the Son into the world for this purpose, that his people might have everlasting life. Those who believe in him are not condemned. Those who don't are condemned already—they've been bitten by the curse and refuse to look at the remedy. Only those who trust him can be saved.

Discuss

- Both Hebrew and Greek use one word for *spirit, wind,* and *breath,* which means 3:8 is intentionally filled with ambiguity and layers of meaning. With that in mind, what do you think Jesus meant when he said that those who are born of the Spirit are like those who are blown by the wind? How have you experienced the Spirit's blowing in your life?

_____

_____

_____

_____

- Why do you think John 3:16 became such a well-known, oft-quoted verse?

  _____

  _____

  _____

  _____

A Case Study

Imagine: You're recognized as one of the foremost Bible scholars of our generation—multiple doctorates, quoted frequently as an expert on CNN, an influential leader in your denomination. But coming out of nowhere onto the religious landscape is a street preacher, attracting throngs who are adamant about the miracles they've seen him do. His teaching seems to strike a chord with the populace, and his works are inexplicable. And because of your status, you're expected to express your opinion.

- How do you go about forming an opinion? Are his miracles enough to convince you he's from God?
- How would you deal with his apparent lack of education? His apparent disregard for well-crafted, long-honored theological views?
- When Larry King asks you what you think of the street preacher, and the nation is listening, how will you respond?
- To what degree does your ego as a respected authority— your sense of territorialism—influence your opinion of this unqualified upstart that everyone seems to be listening to now?

A Surprising Savior

JOHN 4–6

Ancient principles of faith were nonnegotiable. They were embedded in God's law—the everlasting law he gave on Sinai to the dramatic accompaniment of thunder and fire. The curses for falling into such abominable practices as ingesting the blood of meat, for example, or dishonoring the Sabbath, were frightening. Israel had tested God on these issues before and found Jerusalem reduced to rubble and themselves exiled in Babylon. No, God was not playing around with lighthearted suggestions. These were life-and-death issues of obedience.

So what does one do with a miracle-working prophet who seems reckless with Sabbath regulations or who suddenly starts rambling about eating his flesh and drinking his blood? Enjoy

ON WELLS AND WEDDINGS

Those familiar with the Hebrew Scriptures may notice a familiar tone in Jesus's visit to Jacob's well. At least three major characters of the Old Testament found their wives at a well—Isaac (Gen. 24:10–61), Jacob (Gen. 29:1–20), and Moses (Exod. 2:15–22). In each case, the future groom or, in the case of Isaac, his representative, encountered a woman at a well who, after water was drawn, went home to tell others about the encounter. The result was a sojourn with her family and a subsequent betrothal.

In John 3, John the Baptist had called Jesus "the bridegroom." Now Jesus shows up at Jacob's well, where he encounters a woman least likely to be considered "bride material" by most people. Yet Jesus is a different kind of bridegroom, and he's in search of a different kind of bride—those who will believe in him, regardless of their background. The Samaritan woman does exactly that, then, according to precedent, runs off to tell the town about the encounter. Jesus sojourned with them for two days, and many believed in him. It was precisely the kind of betrothal this bridegroom was looking for.

the miracles, but know when it's time to walk away. At least that's the response most people had.

People of faith don't often know what to do with spiritual enigmas, no matter how godly those enigmas might be. Jesus was just such an enigma—still is, in fact, as his Spirit continues to blow where he wishes, regardless of our attempts to systematize his ways. For those who have been Christians for a long time, it should come as no surprise that God is . . . well, very surprising.

How so? Consider the times your prayers have been answered exactly the way you expected them to be; or the people God has brought into your life who have taught you something, challenged you, or surprised you with encouragement; or the great opportunities that have come along precisely when they were supposed to. You may be able to come up with a few examples of these things, but it's probably a very short list. That's because God fits no formulas. He's "outside the box" in virtually everything he does.

That's the Jesus portrayed by John's gospel—enigmatic, surprising, and unconventional. He's worthy of ultimate belief, but few people are able to give it to him at this point in the book. Before John concludes, we'll see all the right declarations about him, of course. But for now, his followers have varying degrees of faith. And by the end of this section, most won't have any faith at all.

The Well: John 4

Focus: John 4:1–42

She had three strikes against her. She was a Samaritan, a loathsome race to pureblood Jews; a woman for whom a conversation alone with a man in public would be deemed inappropriate by most; and a sinner—the kind of woman whose blatant immorality was enough to sully the reputation of any man she spoke to.

The first two strikes wouldn't have bothered the other women of Sychar, but the third would. That's why she was coming to the well at noon. Alone. After all the good wives and daughters had drawn their day's water in the cool of the morning and then taken their sharp tongues and sharper stares back home.

This day there was a stranger at the well. That wasn't unusual. This wasn't just any well; it was Jacob's well, full not only of water but of history and symbolism too. Lots of travelers stopped there—even Galileans who, as much as it pained them, had to pass through Samaria on their way to and from feasts in Jerusalem.

This traveler was a Galilean, in fact, and his request for water was stunning. How could this appeal come from a Jew? Jews considered Samaritans—along with all their eating and drinking utensils—to be unclean. To drink from her water jar would have made him ritually unclean too, at least in the mind of most Jews. But that didn't seem to matter to this one. Apparently, he was there for something other than water—perhaps to meet the kind of woman who would show up alone at a well at noon. It wouldn't be the first time.

But that wasn't the direction in which this traveler took the conversation. No, he made cryptic comments about life-giving water and implied that he knew where to get some. Then he told her to go get her husband.

"I have no husband," she replied—which, whether or not she intended it, sent a clear message: "Yes, I happen to be available." But again, the visitor didn't take the conversation in that direction. He prophesied instead about her past, telling her how many husbands she had had, and pointing out that her current partner was not, in fact, her husband at all. And at this, she began to be impressed. *A holy man*, she thought. She took the opportunity to ask this prophet a pointed religious question to determine whose side he was on. Samaritans, she reminded him, used to worship on nearby Mount Gerizim—that is, until Jews destroyed their temple years before. So whose mountain is the right one?

Jesus assured her that the location of worship wasn't the real issue—that worship is a matter of the heart. He then revealed that he was the Messiah, the *Taheb* the Samaritans had long been waiting for, the restorer prophesied by Moses. And at that, this unlikely woman ran from this unlikely conversation to tell the rest of the town—the people she had been so careful to avoid—about the remarkable stranger she had met at Jacob's well.

"THE PROPHET"

Moses had foretold it long ago. "The LORD your God will raise up for you a prophet like me from among your own brothers. You must listen to him. . . . The LORD said to me: '. . . I will put my words in his mouth, and he will tell them everything I command him. If anyone does not listen to my words that the prophet speaks in my name, I myself will call him to account'" (Deut. 18:15, 17–19).

Messianic expectations, among Jews and Samaritans alike, were bolstered by this prophecy. For centuries, Jews had waited for the Prophet-like-Moses. This was what the priests of Jerusalem had in mind when they went out to inquire of John the Baptist. "Are you the Prophet?" they asked, to which John responded negatively. This was what the Samaritan woman had in mind when she mentioned the Messiah in John 4:25. And this is what the people who witnessed Jesus's miracles had in mind when they remarked in 6:14, "Surely this is the Prophet who is to come into the world." They will say the same in 7:40 upon hearing his teaching. They knew that someone at least as important and life-changing as Moses was among them. After all, they had just been fed with bread as miraculous as manna in the wilderness.

Discuss

- To this point, John has told how Jesus testified of himself to an interested skeptic (Nathanael in 1:43–51), an inquisitive Pharisee (Nicodemus in 3:1–21), and an unsuspecting outcast (the Samaritan in 4:1–42). What does this unlikely assortment of characters tell us about Jesus's ministry?

_____

_____

_____

_____

24

- In what ways does John highlight Jesus's ability to defy expectations in each of these encounters? In what ways has Jesus defied expectations in your life?

_____

_____

_____

_____

The Witnesses: John 5

Focus: John 5:30–46

Since the incident in Sychar, Jesus has performed two more dramatic signs: he healed a secular government official's son (4:46–54)—from a distance—and healed a lame man waiting to get in a pool of "miracle water" (5:1–17)—on the Sabbath. The second of these incidents created quite a stir. Jesus had already broken protocol on several occasions, and now he has broken rabbinic laws of the Sabbath—a law against physicians healing any non-life-threatening malady, and a law against requiring someone to pick up a pallet and walk, which amounts to work. To top it all off, Jesus has called God his personal "Father"—a seemingly preposterous claim of essential equality with God. As a result, he explains his relationship with the Father in more detail—and reasserts his authority in plainer terms.

Now the discussion has degenerated into a legal testimony. The Jewish leaders have plenty of witnesses on their side—including a less-than-grateful beneficiary of a miracle among them (see the interrogation of 5:10–17). In Hebraic law, at least two witnesses were required in a case (5:31), so Jesus begins to call the witnesses for his defense. It's an impressive list: John the Baptist (5:33); his miracles (5:36); the Father himself (5:37); the Scriptures (5:39); and Moses (5:45–46). Case closed.

- Why do you think Jesus's witnesses didn't convince his accusers of his identity? In your experience, what does it take to convince someone that Jesus is who he said he is?

_____

_____

_____

_____

The Walkout: John 6

Focus: John 6:25–70

In the first half of chapter 6, Jesus has fed a multitude. It's the fourth of the seven signs and the only miracle recorded in all four gospels. He immediately follows it up with the fifth sign: walking on water. And when the crowd arrives at the other side of the sea, they marvel that though he hadn't gotten in the boat with the disciples, he made it there anyway.

Having just fed thousands of people in a "wilderness" of sorts, Jesus calls himself the bread of heaven. Or, to put it more accurately, he's the real manna that comes down from heaven, the fulfillment of God's provision in the wilderness between Egypt and the Promised Land. But he's different from that manna, because those who eat of him won't die like their ancestors did. In fact, the bread is his flesh—the "kernel of wheat" that must fall into the ground and die, as he explains in a later chapter. Furthermore, his blood is true wine. Only those who eat the bread of his flesh and drink the wine of his blood can live.

The message doesn't go over well. Few people can stomach such strange teachings, and nearly everyone leaves the miracle worker on account of his absurd claims. It's the low point of his popularity, to be surpassed later only by the shame of his death. Only his disciples—his true disciples, primarily the twelve—

remain. "Where else could we go?" Peter asks. Only Jesus has words of eternal life. Even if they are hard to understand.

Jesus, of course, wasn't speaking of cannibalism—or even of a sacrament he would introduce later. He was speaking of himself as the source of life. "You are what you eat," he might as well have said, and then emphasized a diet of his teaching as nourishment for everlasting life. The Lord's Supper would one day reflect that truth as a visible manifestation of an eternal reality, but the hearers on the far side of the sea couldn't have known that. All they knew was that Jesus's miracles were great, his teaching was filled with confusing symbolism, and his claims were really hard to swallow.

Discuss

- In this session, Jesus has identified himself as "living water" and "bread from heaven." Are you currently experiencing him as the satisfaction of your spiritual hunger and thirst? If so, what encouragement can you give others in your group about how to be filled? If not, what might be hindering your satisfaction in him?

_____

_____

_____

_____

_____

_____

Imagine: There are certain things about church and Christianity you've been taught all your life—which day to worship, how to dress on that day, how to be a good steward of God's resources, how to relate to certain kinds of people . . . and the list goes on. Now you hear about a man who contradicts many of these foundational principles. He can quote a lot of Bible verses, but he certainly sees them through a different lens. In fact, he makes quite a few bold statements about himself that, frankly, seem rather inflated. And, mysteriously, he happens to be helping people in a lot of unexplainable ways.

- In forming your opinion of him, which is stronger: your long-held convictions or the evidence of his power? Why?
- If you searched Scripture and found that he didn't fit your interpretation of it, would you be more inclined to alter your interpretation or declare him a false teacher? Why?
- If hordes of nonreligious people flocked to see his alleged miracles and hear his teaching, would you tend to see him as a passing popular trend or a potentially lasting influence? Why?

Jesus on Trial—Again

JOHN 7–8

A strange movement was sweeping across American Christianity, infecting churches everywhere with its biblically questionable practices. Most churches seemed oblivious to the implications; they were ignorant and indiscriminate, simply going along with the crowd because it seemed like the right thing to do. But those leaders and churches with knowledge of the Scriptures and a true gift of discernment diligently protected themselves against this passing trend. They would have none of that nonsense. They were vigilant about remaining true to New Testament teaching. What was this new movement? Sunday school.

One of the more vocal opponents to the suspicious new movement wrote this about it in a newspaper editorial: "I emphatically deny that there is any divine authority for Sunday

29

schools, either by precept or precedent, hint or allusion. . . . In all the writings of the New Testament there is not one word that even squints in that direction" (J. T. Showalter in the *Gospel Advocate*, April, 1910). A handful of opponents even taught that Sunday school advocates were destined for hell unless they repented.

The fear was that these newfangled "Sunday schools" would put Bible teaching in the hands of uneducated and untrained laypeople, cultivate diverse doctrines through the various curricula they used, and splinter churches in the process. In other words, it would mess up the current order. Plus, there were no specific chapter-and-verse references to Sunday school anywhere in the New Testament. Therefore, it was contrary to Scripture.

The same thing was said of missionary societies during the nineteenth century. "Sit down, young man," said a church elder to William Carey, the father of the modern missionary movement. "If God wants to save the heathen in India, he will do it without your help or mine!" This idea of going to "backward" people and trying to explain the gospel of the kingdom was considered by many to be pointless and potentially threatening. It could even undermine the colonial order.

Sadly, religious people have often opposed the movement of God throughout history. That's because God doesn't fit our expectations, and he sometimes upsets the balance of institutions and their leaders, threatening the status quo. And for those who are attached to the status quo, that's a problem—especially when they believe God put the status quo in place to begin with.

That's the scene in John 7–8 and throughout the rest of the gospel. It's an epic clash of kingdoms, a vigorous battle between light and darkness, good and evil, truth and lies. Jesus comes into Jerusalem and makes a big splash, upsetting the power base and the religious order of the scribes, priests, and teachers

JESUS AT THE FEASTS

Most of the events and dialogue in the gospel of John take place during the feasts of Israel: a Passover in chapters 2–3; the Feast of Trumpets (most likely), also known as Rosh Hashanah, in chapter 5; another Passover in chapter 6; the Feast of Tabernacles in chapters 7–10; Hanukkah in the second half of chapter 10; and another Passover in chapters 12–20. John's selection of these events and discourses is purposeful. It's a way of saying that Israel's feasts pointed forward to the Messiah, that he's the fulfillment of all of their symbolism and meaning. John highlights how the substance of Jesus fills the form of God-ordained rituals and, in fact, overshadows them just as a building overshadows its original blueprints.

of the law. They weren't going to allow any uneducated, rule-breaking Galilean with rumors swirling about him to mess up their system. So they opposed him. And God. They missed the time of their visitation.

We often face similar tension between the Spirit and the status quo today—individually and corporately. The issue we have to deal with is how to determine when something is from God and when it isn't. And, as with the early opponents of Sunday school, our perception of what God is doing might be too narrow. We have to be more than knowledgeable about the Word; we have to be sensitive to the Spirit who breathed it.

As Messiah: John 7

Focus: John 7:25–44

In John 2, Jesus's mother urged him to do something about the lack of wine at a wedding feast. Jesus told her his time had not yet come, but then he did something about the situation.

31

In John 7, his brothers urge him to go to Jerusalem for a feast, and he responds the same way: his time has not yet come. But then he goes to the feast anyway—covertly, at first, before creating quite a stir.

It's the Feast of Tabernacles, a celebration marked with water and lights. The festival began with the lighting of giant lamp-stands in a torch ceremony and a declaration that God shone his light on Israel. Then every morning of the weeklong feast, a priest would walk to the nearby Gihon spring, fill a golden

"I AM"

When Moses asked for God's name in Exodus 3:13, God responded with "I AM." The Hebrew word YHWH (or YHVH)—from which we get Yahweh and Jehovah—is mysterious and was never used as an expression for "I am," but that's the closest meaning it has. That's why many believe that when Jesus said, "Before Abraham was, I am," he was using the sacred name of God for himself. That connotation would also apply, to a lesser extent, to his many other "I am" statements in John.

Some scholars disagree that Jesus could have used the divine name in 8:58 because it wasn't grammatically usable and wouldn't have made sense. They argue that the offense of Jesus's statement was due to the fact that it made him out to be pre-existent to Abraham and therefore greater than him. But the gospel of John is written in Greek, and it uses the same words for "I am" in John 8:38 that the Greek translation of Hebrew Scripture used for God's name in Exodus 3:13—*ego eimi*. So Jesus's actual Aramaic or Hebrew expression is buried under the Greek of the gospel and remains unknown to us. If Jesus *had* spoken the divine name, however, it would have to be translated just as we see it in our Bibles today: "I am."

Regardless of the words Jesus actually used, we can be certain of one thing: whatever he said, it was blasphemous enough in the minds of the religious leaders to cause them to pick up stones to kill him immediately.

pitcher with water, carry it back into the temple, and pour it at the base of the altar. It was an expression of gratitude for the rain that produced the harvest and a prayer for future rain. One of the Scripture verses quoted in connection with this ceremony, which climaxed on the last day of the feast, was Isaiah 12:3: "With joy you will draw water from the wells of salvation."

On the last day of this feast, after a week of controversy and public confrontation with religious leaders and wavering crowds, Jesus watches the priest raise the pitcher of water and pour it out. The gathered crowds sing a hymn of praise, after which is silence. At this climactic moment, it is believed, Jesus stands up and shouts loudly: "If anyone is thirsty, let him come to me and drink. Whoever believes in me, as the Scripture has said, streams of living water will flow from within him" (7:37–38).

All eyes are on Jesus. His declaration of his identity could be no clearer than this. And for those who have witnessed this scene, neutrality is no longer an option. Either he is telling the truth and worthy of honor as Messiah, or he is a lying blasphemer and worthy of death. Predictably, his declaration splits the crowd. Some believe he is the Prophet or the Christ (for some this is one and the same), and others want him arrested. But because his time has not yet come, he cannot be touched.

Discuss

- Why do you think the religious leaders were so zealously opposed to Jesus? How would their lives have changed if they had simply believed him?

  _____

  _____

  _____

  _____

33

- Jesus spoke of streams of living water (the Spirit) flowing from within those who believe. What do you think that's supposed to look like in a believer's life?

_____

_____

_____

_____

_____

_____

As God: John 8

Focus: John 8:12, 31–38, 48–59

Still at the feast—John 8:1–11 seems to be an insertion of an episode from earlier or later that week—Jesus declares himself to be the light of the world, probably in the presence of the shining lampstands that were lit on day one. Those who believe in him, he says, will never walk in darkness.

Bold statements like this cause the confrontation with authorities to continue, and it only gets more acrimonious. At one point, Jesus turns from those opposing him and declares to those who believe that the truth will set them free. The enemies scoff. They've never been slaves, they declare. But Jesus insists that they are, in reality, slaves of sin. The fact that they are descendants of Abraham doesn't change that, and it doesn't automatically make them receptive to the truth. "You have no room for my word," he tells them.

The discussion of Abraham leads to another climactic moment. Jesus tells these descendants of Abraham that their patriarch rejoiced to see his day. How has he seen Abraham? His answer, if untrue, is a greater blasphemy than any yet spoken: "Before Abraham was, I am."

34

Discuss

- In what ways does Jesus bring us into the light and set us free? How would you describe the darkness and captivity you once lived in, and how do the light and freedom of Jesus contrast with your life before knowing Him?

  _____

  _____

  _____

  _____

  _____

- Why didn't the authorities' knowledge of Scripture enable them to see the truth about Jesus? What criteria can we use to discern a true movement of God?

  _____

  _____

  _____

  _____

  _____

A Case Study

Imagine: You're at a Fourth of July parade in a small town, and you're enjoying watching the numerous floats and banners and bands pass by—all of them, of course, celebrating the theme of freedom. When the last entry in the parade finally enters the town square, the mayor walks up to the platform to begin his welcome speech. But in the brief moment before he utters a word, a voice pierces the silence. It's the same guy from the case study in the last session standing up and yelling at the top of his lungs. "Anyone who follows me will discover what real freedom is all about!"

- How do you react internally to someone who would create such a scene? Theatrics aside, how do you react to someone who says such things about himself?
- How would you expect the police and other authorities at the event to respond?
- Are there any circumstances that could have occurred—any previous experiences with this man—that might cause you to be sympathetic to his loud declaration? If so, what?
- Does this example change how you view Jesus or the crowd and authorities in John 7–8? Why or why not?

Light in Darkness

JOHN 9–10

"I'm serious, Dan. God healed her when that evangelist preached at that revival I went to," Sue told her husband. "She's walking around now. I've seen her."

"Did you know her before that?" Dan answered. "Have you ever seen her in a wheelchair?"

"No, not personally. I only met her a couple weeks ago when she gave her testimony. But I know people who say she was paralyzed for years."

"And you trust their word? I've seen this before, Sue—no one has witnessed the miracle personally, but everyone says they know people who have. Then you ask those people, and they say they got their information secondhand too. There's never anyone to verify it."

Sue sighed. "But that's not what happened here. I have trust-worthy friends who say she was in a wheelchair one minute, then the preacher prayed for her, and she got out of the wheelchair and has been walking ever since."

"How do they know she wasn't planted there by the evan-gelist's team—a prearranged 'healing'?"

"Why are you so suspicious, Dan? Why can't you just believe it was a miracle?"

"Because I've heard what that preacher teaches. He says some strange things that don't line up with Scripture. So if he's a false teacher, it's a false miracle, right? It has to be. He isn't from God."

ABOUT "THE JEWS"

Throughout the book of John, Jesus gets vehement opposition from a group called "the Jews." But in light of the fact that Jesus, his disciples, the sympathetic crowds, and witnesses such as John the Baptist and the prophets who went before were all Jews, how does this designation make sense? If all the people in the discussion are Jews, why single out "the Jews"?

The answer lies in the translation of *Ioudaios*. It *could* simply mean Jews, but it's more likely that John is referring to Judean leaders—the branch of Judaism that was concentrated in Jerusalem; that dominated the priest-hood and governance of the nation; that considered itself purebred, faithful experts on the law; and that considered Galilean Jews, Samaritans, and the common crowds in Judea ignorant and gullible. And, in fact, this attitude shows up clearly in chapters 7–10 (see 7:47–49 and 9:34, for example). "The Jews"—i.e., the majority of the Judean priesthood—considered them-selves the guardians of God's Word and held all others in pious contempt. But by no means were Jews in general as uniformly opposed to Jesus as the English translation of this word might imply.

"But Dan, there's plenty of solid testimony that it *was* a miracle. My close friends—your friends too—swear to it. How could that happen if God didn't do it?"

"I don't know, Sue. Maybe Satan did it to deceive people like you."

"You're accusing him of being demonic?"

"Well, it's possible. You know what Jesus said about false teachers doing signs and wonders to deceive even the elect. But really, Sue, it's much more likely that he's simply a fraud. All I know is things just don't add up."

Reports of modern-day miracles are plentiful, but skepticism about them remains high. And those reports often lead to conversations like the one above—at least internally in our own mind, if not actually discussed with others. Those who want to believe in the power of God are afraid of being gullible. And for those who don't want to believe, the true skeptics, there's never enough proof. The evidence is always shaky, the witnesses unreliable, the motives for deception far too obvious—even when they aren't.

That's exactly the kind of theological dilemma that the religious leaders and crowds of Jerusalem found themselves in. Jesus's foes were confounded by his miracles. They tried to pick apart the evidence, to strip the witnesses of reliability, even to speculate about demonic influence and deceptive motives behind his acts. The most obvious answer—that God had actually done a miracle—seemed too improbable for some of them to even consider. So those who were skeptical from the start couldn't see the truth and missed God. But those who sincerely sought the truth were given the eyes of faith to find it.

39

SHEEP, VOICES, AND GATES

Jesus's example of sheep recognizing their master's voice is rooted in reality. It's true that shepherds use a distinctive voice with their own sheep, and mixed flocks will in fact separate when they hear their shepherd's call and follow him.

It's also true that in the Middle East, shepherds often sleep with their body lying across the opening in the wall of the sheep pen, making themselves the actual gate that keeps their sheep in at night. So when Jesus spoke of himself as the door, he was painting a picture of his self-sacrificing desire to keep his sheep together and safe from predators.

An Indisputable Witness: John 9

He had been blind all his life. That, according to the spiritual culture of the day, was more than simply an unfortunate birth defect. It was the wages of sin—somebody's, whether those of the blind man himself, his parents, or even his grandparents. Scripture was clear—well, except for those exceptions like Joseph and Job—that obedience is accompanied by blessing, and disobedience is accompanied by a curse. And blindness is definitely evidence of cursedness. A man reduced to begging by the road is obviously not under the favor of God.

So the disciples ask Jesus about this man, whether it was his sins or his parents' sins that caused his blindness. A lot was hanging on this answer; if it was the man's own sin, it would point to the possibility of sin *in utero* because he had been blind since birth. But Jesus doesn't answer their either/or question. And he doesn't even give the theologically sophisticated reason that this happened because we live in a fallen world and that sin, in general, has resulted in this kind of infirmity, without a one-to-one correlation.

No, there's a deeper reason. This man was born blind in order for God to demonstrate his glory. His healing would become an eternal testimony to the compassion and power of Jesus.

And it's true; Jesus's glory is revealed. But again, it creates quite a furor. Maybe this isn't the same man who was blind, some speculate. Others are convinced that he is. The parents are brought into the discussion. Yes, this is their son, they say; and yes, he was born blind. Beyond that, they won't speak. It's a fearful thing to stand in the way of religious authorities on a mission. "You'll have to ask him how it happened," they say. "We have no comment."

Still, unlike the healed paralytic in chapter 5, this man doesn't waver. The inquisitors can decide what they want to do about Jesus, but the fact remains that a miracle occurred. There was blindness, then sight. All signs point to God, he says, which earns him a strong rebuke from these educated spiritual leaders who don't value the opinion of a beggar so obviously sinful from birth. And in rejecting the man's miracle of sight, they persist in their own blindness.

Discuss

- How common today do you think is the belief that trials are the direct result of sin? What is the biblical evidence both for and against this idea?

  _____

  _____

  _____

  _____

- In what ways might you benefit from seeing your needs as opportunities for God to demonstrate his glory rather

41

than as problems to suffer through? How might he demonstrate his glory in them?

_____

_____

_____

_____

The Shepherd's Voice: John 10

Focus: John 10:1–21

Jesus comments on the controversy that has just taken place. He puts his ongoing conflict with the religious authorities in some very recognizable terms for his followers. Shepherds and sheep were not only familiar fixtures in an agrarian economy; they were also images used by the prophets quite often to portray Israel's leaders and its people. So when Jesus starts talking about those who enter the sheep pen, his listeners know the terms of the parable.

There are actually three parables or metaphors blended into this discussion. The first is in verses 1–6. It portrays the people of God as sheep in a pen and Jesus as their shepherd. The watchman, John the Baptist, opens the gate for him, and those who know him listen to his voice—i.e., obey him and follow him. They won't follow after strangers, those false teachers of Israel who have been opposing his teaching. Real sheep recognize the voice of their master, who knows them individually by name.

This parable confuses Jesus's followers, so he tells another in verses 7–10. This time, Jesus is the gate to the pen, and the destination of the sheep is the pasture outside the pen—true life in the kingdom of God. The religious leaders opposing Jesus are thieves and robbers trying to lead God's sheep astray. They don't come in through the gate, and they don't lead sheep out through the gate. They break down the walls of the pen, desiring nothing but to steal, kill, and destroy the sheep. The true gate is the only way for the sheep to have real life and live it to the fullest.

Then in verses 11–16, Jesus the Good Shepherd forecasts his sacrifice. He will lay down his life for the sheep—unlike the hired hands, who will abandon their job when the wolf, the enemy of God's sheep, comes near. The Good Shepherd knows his sheep—even those beyond the fold of Israel who have not yet been shepherded—and he will sacrifice his life for all of them.

The sum effect of these blended metaphors about shepherds and sheep is a message about Jesus's intentions. It's his way of saying about his opponents, "I care for you; they don't." He's the one who is actually concerned for the welfare of the sheep, while the leaders are concerned primarily for their positions.

Discuss

- There are a lot of voices competing for our attention, both within Christendom and beyond it. What are some ways to sort out the ones that represent our Shepherd from the ones that don't?

_____

_____

_____

_____

- How does our Shepherd speak? In what situations has he spoken to you?

_____

_____

_____

_____

A CASE STUDY

Imagine: You've prayed this prayer for years: "Lord, you know how long I've suffered from this sickness. You know how desperately I've prayed again and again that you'd remove it. I've learned to trust you in it, I've learned patience, and I've learned to endure. But I don't know what else there is to learn. And I can't imagine why you wouldn't want to deliver me from it now. I know you aren't ignoring me, but it seems from all appearances that you are. Lord, please . . . what are you waiting for? Why won't you help me?"

- Who or what is the subject of this prayer? Whose perspective does it reflect?
- How would your prayer change if God revealed that he wanted to use your deliverance for his glory at a specific time? Whose perspective would your prayer then reflect?
- In what ways might God use this situation for his glory?

Lord of Life

JOHN 11–12

"If only they could see a miracle, they would believe!" Most Christians have thought that about someone they know and love. We want God to give more evidence for himself, to show up in a way that can't be denied. Then faith will come naturally for those who witness his power.

Is that true, though? The answer is yes. And no. And sort of. We see all kinds of responses to Jesus's miracles in the gospel of John. It all depends on the person. Some saw and believed on account of the signs (2:23; 4:53; 10:42; 11:45). Some refused to believe in spite of seeing signs (7:5; 10:25–26; 12:37). And some remained on the fence; they saw signs and asked for more signs because they still weren't sure (6:30). Jesus makes it clear that faith is more than an intellectual opinion. "No one can come to me unless the Father who sent him draws him" (6:44).

At the end of the gospel, Thomas, the disciple who doubted, insisted on seeing Jesus before believing he had been raised from the dead. And though Jesus let him see and touch the wounds of his resurrected body, he followed up Thomas's worship with his view on seeing and believing: "Blessed are those who have not seen me and yet have believed" (20:29).

Christians have already come to that place of belief without having seen Jesus in the flesh, but we still waver sometimes. We aren't always sure God is going to provide for our needs or answer our prayers until he has encouraged us with several answers already, and even then our faith is often stretched. We vacillate between needing evidence for our faith and realizing

CAIAPHAS

Caiaphas was the high priest between AD 18–36. As a Sadducee, he rejected the idea of any kind of resurrection or afterlife, which would have made Jesus's talk about resurrection seem ludicrous to him. And as a brutally pragmatic politician, he would have been particularly harsh on anyone at the center of Jerusalem's messianic frenzy. That's because Rome allowed Jewish provinces to function in relative freedom only when stability was maintained. If things got out of control, the empire would step in with its own form of control. And if Jesus ever became the populist messiah of Judea . . . well, that would amount to a revolt in the eyes of Rome. The repercussions would be catastrophic.

So the status quo was more than just a preference for Caiaphas. It was necessary for the political survival of the nation. And for a cold political pragmatist under Rome's watch, sacrificing one troublemaking "messiah" in order to save the temple, the priesthood, and some semblance of self-governance made perfect sense.

that faith is defined as believing what we don't see. And Jesus understands. He gives us testimonies from the past (such as the gospel of John and the rest of Scripture) and the present (those around us who tell how they've experienced God). He gives us promises about answering our prayers and then answers them. He surrounds us with encouragement that we can sense without seeing. He teaches us, step by step, to walk by faith and not by sight.

That, essentially, is the path the disciples have been on in John, and the journey comes to a head in this session. Jesus's miraculous works become so "in your face" that neutrality has to be abandoned for belief or rejection. And when the crowds and leaders are forced to form their opinion, the stage is set for history's most critical moment of truth at one Passover in Jerusalem.

Resurrection Preview: John 11

Focus: John 11:1–44

The news comes to Jesus and his disciples that a beloved friend is sick. Jesus assures them that Lazarus's illness won't *end* in death—not mentioning, of course, that death would come in the *middle* of the story. Still, Jesus has no sense of urgency about the matter. After two days, he tells the disciples it's time to go—and that Lazarus is now dead. And it's best, Jesus says, that he wasn't there when it happened.

The disciples' confusion must have paled in comparison to Mary's and Martha's, the sisters of Lazarus. They each tell Jesus, somewhat pointedly, that if he had been there, Lazarus would not have died. It's a complaint nearly everyone has made to God at some point: "Where were you when I needed you?" Jesus weeps with them in their sadness and comforts them with

THE BOOK OF SIGNS

With the raising of Lazarus, the "book of signs" portion of John concludes. The seven signs were:

Water into wine (2:1–11)
Healing of the official's son (4:43–54)
Sabbath healing of the lame man (5:1–18)
Feeding of the five thousand (6:1–15)
Walking on water (6:16–21)
Sabbath healing of the blind man (9:1–41)
Raising of Lazarus (11:1–44)

John places much emphasis throughout his gospel on how the signs relate to belief. He concludes the "book of signs" with two key statements: "Many of the Jews who had come to visit Mary, and had seen what Jesus did, put their faith in him" (11:45); and, "Here is this man performing many miraculous signs. If we let him go on like this, everyone will believe in him" (11:47–48). The signs were polarizing, causing some to believe more deeply, and others to oppose him even more vigorously.

An eighth sign is still to come, of course—the resurrection of Jesus. Interestingly, the number seven in Scripture often symbolizes perfection, completeness, and resurrection, and eight represents new beginnings. The seven signs are completed with a resurrection; and the ultimate sign, the eighth, signifies the ultimate new beginning.

assurances about the resurrection. In fact, he tells them, he *is* the resurrection. And they are about to see the glory of God.

Verse 38 indicates that Jesus is somewhat angry—"troubled," according to most translations—at how death has so painfully intruded on his creation. He orders the stone removed from the grave, to which Martha objects. It has been four days, after all, and the stench would be overwhelming. But there's design in the timing; rabbinic writings indicate a belief that a person's spirit hovered over his or her body for three days after death and then departed, after which there could be no hope of resuscitation. And "hopeless" seems to have been Jesus's desire from the beginning of the story. That's why he's glad he waited until after Lazarus had died and why he says in his prayer that people will believe in him on account of what's about to happen. Only a truly "hopeless" miracle will be enough to convince some people of who he is.

After his prayer, Jesus shouts. Loudly. And life miraculously fills Lazarus's dead body once again. Bound tightly in burial wrappings, he comes stumbling out of the tomb to the amazement of everyone. All that remains is to strip the death clothes off of this risen man and welcome him back to the land of the living.

Discuss

- When have you experienced a seemingly callous delay in God's answer to your prayers? What was your relationship with God like during that time? Has the situation been resolved?

  _____

  _____

  _____

  _____

- Why do you think Jesus prefers to work in impossible situations?

  _____

  _____

  _____

  _____

The Jesus Problem: John 12

Focus: John 12:1–36

The days after Lazarus came out of the tomb were tumultuous. The Jewish authorities convened an emergency meeting to
discuss the Jesus problem. It had become more than a matter
of jealousy and spite; local stability was the key to keeping the
Romans at a distance. The high priest, Caiaphas, recognized
this very real threat, leading him to utter one of Scripture's most
unintentionally accurate prophecies: "It is better for you that
one man die for the people than that the whole nation perish"
(11:50). So from that day forward, the Judeans plotted to kill
Jesus, even issuing an "all points bulletin" for his whereabouts
(11:57).

Now some time later, Jesus has returned to Bethany and
is eating with Mary, Martha, and Lazarus. In another pro-
phetic statement, Mary brings a vessel of very expensive nard,
an amount of fragrant oil worth a year's wages, and poured it
over Jesus. In the opinion of the treasurer, Judas, this is a huge
waste of resources. But Jesus knows—the long-awaited hour is
about to come. This anointing is for his upcoming burial.

Meanwhile, the news of the Lazarus miracle has spread.
Crowds seek for a touch from Jesus and a glimpse of the living dead man. And because Lazarus is now "exhibit A" in the
case for Jesus's divinity, he becomes the target of a death plot
too. Erasing such convincing evidence would certainly help the
prosecution's cause.

As the time of Passover approaches, Jesus enters Jerusalem
for the last time amid the shouts and praises of the people. His
popularity, so weak in chapter 6, has now risen to unprecedented
heights—as has his opposition. He knows that "the hour" that
had not yet come so many times in John has now come. It is

time for God to glorify his name; for the prince of this world to be cast out; and for the Son of Man to be lifted up.

Discuss

- If you were faced with a choice between your country's national security and the presence of Jesus, which would you choose? What do you think you would have done if you were one of Judea's leaders during his ministry?

  _____

  _____

  _____

  _____

- It's easy to see how 12:24 applies to Jesus. What does it mean for you both to love your life and hate your life (v. 25)?

  _____

  _____

  _____

  _____

51

A CASE STUDY

Imagine: You've been at a loved one's bedside for days, helplessly watching life slip away. At first your prayers were full of faith that God would heal, but now your faith is weak. You've seen the steady decline. Your prayers don't seem to be working—that's clear. For whatever reason, for some excruciating mystery behind God's will, he's letting your loved one—and you—suffer extreme pain.

- Does your faith in God's intervention rise and fall with the difficulty of a situation like this? How is that contrary to the way Jesus worked in John 11?
- How do you think God would respond if your faith grew stronger as the situation worsened? How do you think the people around you would respond?
- How important is it to you to have others understand and respect your faith? How might that desire get in the way of believing God for impossible things?

Secrets of the Heart

JOHN 13–16

The old craftsman knew his time was running out. He had spent a lifetime earning his reputation as the finest maker of stringed instruments ever. His violins and cellos were eagerly sought by the greatest virtuosos in the world. But his hands had already made their last instrument. His illness had progressed too far.

His artistry would live on, however. For years, he had trained his sons in his craft. They knew all the technical aspects of the work; there was no need—or time—for any further instruction about that. No, in the little time he had before he would breathe his last breath, it would be more important for this artisan to pass on the secrets of his heart: how he was motivated not by monetary gain or even the beauty of a fine instrument but by the

THE INCARNATIONAL V

John 13 is a graphic picture of the incarnation, something akin to an artist's masterful portrait of a timeless truth. The truth it represents is explained in the gospel's prologue: "In the beginning was the Word, and the Word was with God, and the Word was God. . . . The Word became flesh and made his dwelling among us. . . . From the fullness of his grace we have all received one blessing after another" (John 1:1, 14, 16). It's what Jesus refers to with every mention of where he came from and where he's going. It's the great descent from the throne of heaven to the lowlands of the earth—including an ignominious burial within it—and it ends with ultimate exaltation.

For a fascinating parallel, read Philippians 2:5–11, an early hymn that portrays the same V-shaped trajectory of Jesus's incarnation. He took off the clothes of heaven, donned the garb of a servant, gave his life, and was re-clothed in honor and highly exalted. And don't forget the practical application: in both John 13 and Philippians 2, followers of Jesus are told to take the same trajectory in their lives. Life, servanthood and sacrifice, death, and resurrection. This is the biography of those who truly belong to him.

beauty of the music it could produce; how the technical skills of making instruments were only half of the process and the heart that went into them mattered just as much; how a true craftsman can breathe life into wood and strings. These were the more important lessons. He had already tried to teach them to his sons, but only a few more days remained—even hours, perhaps—for him to drive those lessons home.

Last words reveal a lot about a person's deepest values. They carry much more weight than normal conversations. That's because when time is short, priorities move to the forefront. Whatever message a departing person wants to leave behind takes center stage at the end.

Jesus had only a few more hours with his disciples, so he filled those hours with critical teaching. John 13–16 contain some of the most intensely powerful messages in all of Scripture. This section is dense with rich material about love, servanthood, prayer, suffering, heaven, and the Holy Spirit. Jesus offers his disciples much encouragement and gives them precious promises that they will need as his followers after he's gone. He tells them they will be like him—in power, in love, and in suffering. And best of all, they won't be left alone. His own Spirit will not only be with them but will enter into them. Their relationship with him will continue to deepen forever.

In the Form of a Servant: John 13

Jesus does a remarkable thing during his last meal with his disciples. He takes off his garments and then wraps a towel around his waist. Wearing a servant's clothes and acting out a servant's gestures, he pours water into a basin and washes the feet of his disciples—including the feet of the betrayer who will soon leave the room. Peter has already confessed that Jesus is the Messiah, so he naturally objects to having his feet washed by someone with such higher status. But Jesus spells out what's at stake: those who don't allow the one who came down from heaven to come down even further and cleanse them can't belong to him. After finishing his task, Jesus again takes off the servant's clothes and puts his own robes—including his prayer shawl, naturally—back on. This, he tells them, is the attitude they should have toward one another.

After the betrayer leaves, Jesus gives his disciples a new commandment: to love each other in the same way that he has loved them. Little do they know, at this point, what exactly that entails. But sacrificial love is to become the mark of his followers. That's the only way the world will recognize them—and him in them.

Discuss

- Do you think Christians are known today primarily for our sacrificial love? Why or why not? What are we most known for?

  _____

  _____

  _____

  _____

- How, practically, can we follow Jesus's example of washing each other's feet?

  _____

  _____

  _____

  _____

Peace, Love, Joy, and Persecution: John 14–16

Focus: John 14:1–7, 12–21; 15:1–17; 16:7–15

"Do not let your heart be troubled" (14:1). Jesus promises that he and his disciples will end up in exactly the same place—he uses marriage terminology to make the point—and it will be wonderful.

"I am the way and the truth and the life" (14:6). No one can come to God without coming through Jesus. He is the one who goes to the Father. There are no other ways.

"Anyone who has faith in me will do what I have been doing. He will do even greater things than these, because I am going to

THE TRUE VINE

At the end of chapter 14, Jesus says "let us leave." One can imagine him and the disciples getting up from their meal and, on their way to the Garden of Gethsemane, looking at the object of their discussion: a vine. Israel is frequently portrayed as a vine or vineyard in Hebrew Scriptures (Isa. 5:1–7 and 27:2–4; Ezek. 19:10–14; Ps. 80:8–16). So when Jesus says in 15:1 that he is the *true* vine, he's declaring himself to be the true Israel—*and* that anyone that remains as a branch on that vine is a member of the Israel of God.

Much of John's testimony has led up to this statement. Jesus's wine took the place of ritual purification water and his healings superseded Sabbath restrictions. Soon, he will become the sacrificial lamb for Passover. The Jewish faith and the nation of Israel find their fulfillment in this true vine that God has planted—as do all Jews and Gentiles who come to him in faith.

the Father" (14:12). Jesus assures them that he has been doing the works of God as a human being with faith, not as a special case that no one can emulate. How is this possible? Through prayer, love and obedience, and the power of the Holy Spirit who will reside in those who believe.

"I am the vine; you are the branches" (15:5). This is the key to fruitfulness, for apart from Jesus, his disciples can do nothing. It's also the key to prayer and to revealing the Father's glory through fruitfulness.

"If they persecuted me, they will persecute you also" (15:20). The spirit of Jesus and the world flow in opposite directions. To choose one is to choose against the other. Those who choose Jesus will suffer consequences—though the suffering pales in comparison to the benefits. He, after all, has overcome the world (16:33).

"The Spirit will take from what is mine and make it known to you" (16:15). He will convict of sin, guide into truth, counsel, protect and defend, and disclose future events.

"Your joy will be complete" (16:24). The love that disciples have for one another, the answered prayers we receive, and the fellowship we have with the Spirit will result in more than fruitfulness and the Father's glory. They will result in joy.

Discuss

- Read 14:15, 23–24, and 15:10. What is the relationship between love and obedience?

  _____

  _____

  _____

  _____

- In light of 15:11, how would you respond to someone who says, "God doesn't promise to make you happy"? What's the difference, if any, between happiness and joy?

  _____

  _____

  _____

  _____

- Read 16:7–15. Which, if any, of the works of the Spirit have you experienced in your life? Which ones do you need to experience most right now?

  _____

  _____

  _____

  _____

A Case Study

Imagine: Because of a fortunate relationship with a friend of Europe's richest king, you've been invited to a private gathering of royalty and other VIPs. The royal limo picks you up and drives you through the countryside to the grounds of an enormous castle. The royal guards and servants escort you up the massive stairs leading to the massive doors, which open before you as you approach. As you enter, you see extravagance and opulence beyond your wildest imagination. You're invited to stand in an exclusive reception line, by which the king will be passing soon in order to greet his guests. After a short wait, the king, arrayed in his finest clothes and ornamented with finest jewels and crown, arrives to the blast of loud, festive fanfare. You watch as he nears your spot in the line, and as soon as he sees you, he stops. He immediately takes off his royal coat, trades it for the simple white robe of one of his attendants, bows down before you, and tells you how honored he is that you've come. Then he grabs a tray and begins serving you drinks and hors d'oeuvres, insisting that only his food will nourish you well.

- Knowing who he is and who you are, how awkward does this make you feel? Why might such a generous gesture embarrass you?
- Once it was made clear that this was a required part of anyone's first visit to the castle, with what attitude would you accept the king's service? Would his unconventional welcome be more likely to create humility or arrogance in you? Why?
- In what ways does this scenario reflect your relationship with Jesus?

Clash of Kingdoms

JOHN 17–19

What do Palestine, Chechnya, Kashmir, Rwanda, and the Balkans have in common? At various times in the last few years, each has been the subject of a bitter dispute. The surface issue in each is either the possession of or dominance within a territory. Beneath the surface lies a deeper issue: which culture will have its agenda fulfilled?

Tensions run particularly high over cultural issues because culture—ethnicity, language, beliefs, values, traditions, etc.—shapes our core identity, and our sense of fulfillment hinges on whether our identity is constrained by other forces or freely allowed to thrive. And when two cultures with strong agendas for self-fulfillment compete for the same territory, things can get pretty messy.

The gospels give us a picture of a clash of cultures. It's the agenda of this world for self-fulfillment versus the agenda of the kingdom of God. And yes, it gets very messy. The battle seems to climax when the King of Heaven is slaughtered by the princes of the earth. The collusion between leaders representing Jews and Gentiles appears to express the sentiments of all of humanity: "our agenda must be fulfilled." But in so doing, the agenda of the kingdom is fulfilled, and the battle swings decisively in the other direction.

Where do you stand in the crossfire between those two agendas? While most of us will never join a mob in a public forum and declare which king we want to follow, as at the trial of Jesus, we daily declare our allegiance by our actions and attitudes in the course of ordinary life. In everything we think, say, and do, we are aligning ourselves with someone's agenda: our own, someone else's, or the kingdom of God's. And, as in war and politics, only one agenda can rule the territory of our lives.

John 17

Sometime between his betrayal and his arrest, Jesus prays as the high priest for his people. As the divine mediator between God and humanity, he appeals to the Father on behalf of those who believe in him—not just those who believe now, but all who will believe in the future. And during this remarkable prayer, he makes some astounding statements.

One of Jesus's most surprising requests is that his disciples throughout history be united as one with each other and with him just as he and the Father are one (17:11, 21–22). The prayer for unity is not surprising, but the depth of that unity is shocking. Essentially, he is inviting believers into the Trinity—not as a fourth member, of course, but as part of who Jesus is. We are "in him." The perfect fellowship between Father, Son, and Spirit from eternity past is the model for our relationship with Jesus and with each other. That's amazing.

61

GLORY

Glory is a frequent theme in John. "We have seen his glory," the prologue tells us (1:14), and then John elaborates on the subject throughout the book. It's the Son who glorifies the Father (14:13), and the Father also glorifies the Son (8:54); they glory in each other (13:31–32). And then, remarkably, the Son shares his glory—the glory he received from his Father—with those who love him. And we, in turn, can glorify God through what we say and do (15:8; 21:19).

But what exactly is glory? It seems that it can only be described, not defined. God's glory includes his splendor, honor, majesty, brilliance, and goodness. The Hebrew word for glory, *kabod*, implies the weightiness of these things. And when Scripture speaks of God or Jesus being glorified, it's usually referring to a revealing of his essential character. In other words, the glory and glorification of God means pulling back the curtain on the overwhelming weight of who he is in all of his splendor, honor, majesty, brilliance, and goodness. And that, according to Jesus, is what he willingly shares with those who love him.

Another startling request is that his followers might have the full measure of his joy within them (17:13). The writer of Hebrews tells us that Jesus went to the cross for the joy set before him (Heb. 12:3)—i.e., for the eternal blessing and rewards of exaltation and fellowship with his bride. That unbridled, overwhelming joy is the same joy he plans to share with us. Infinite delight poured out into finite hearts.

Finally, Jesus gives believers the glory that his Father gave him (17:22). God had made it clear in Isaiah 42:8 and 48:11 that he does not share his glory with another—the context implying another rival or an idol. But believers in Jesus are apparently not "another." We are one with him in the same way that he is one with the Father. We are in the holy family. His glory is our glory, and ours is his.

62

Discuss

- How does it encourage you to know that Jesus prayed this prayer for you? In what way might this prayer change how you live?

  _____

  _____

John 18

Focus: John 18:12–40

As Peter stands in the courtyard warming his hands by a fire, he is asked if he is a disciple of Jesus—the rabbi who has said "I am" so often in his ministry. But Peter's response is a lie and a contradiction to the "I am." "I am not," he says. Three times, in fact. The denial foretold by Jesus, but which Peter thought so absurd, has come to pass.

Meanwhile, Jesus is being passed from priest to procurator in fraudulent interrogations and trials. In the process, he affirms that he is a king, but not the kind Pilate would need to worry about. He came into this world to be a witness to truth, and those who love truth recognize him and obey him. Pilate scoffs at the idea, but he has heard what he needs to know. This teacher is certainly no threat to Rome. And though Pilate was willing to set him free, Jesus's Judean opponents preferred to release a rebel.

Discuss

- How inhibited do you feel when it comes to confessing Jesus in public? Why?

  _____

  _____

THE WORTHY FOR THE UNWORTHY

Jesus, the Son of the Father, was condemned while Barabbas (literally, "son of the father") was released. This Bar-abbas—no one knows his given name—had taken part in a rebellion and had a notorious reputation (Matt. 17:16). He was more than a common thief; Luke 23:19 says he was an insurrectionist guilty of murder. The irony is that the true Son of the Father was accused of fomenting a rebellion, though he was innocent; and this unknown "son of the father," though guilty, was declared innocent. But it's more than irony: it's a picture of our salvation. A perfectly righteous life was exchanged for our unrighteousness; he died in our place; and we've been set free. Caiaphas was right. It *is* expedient that one should die for the many.

John 19

Focus: John 19:1–22, 38–42

Pilate doesn't understand the issues surrounding Jesus's "crimes," so he tries to let the situation fizzle out. It won't. The stakes are too high. In a bizarre twist of irony, the Roman representative, Pilate, is found to be an advocate (albeit half-hearted) for the Jewish Messiah; and the Jewish authorities claim that they have "no king but Caesar" (19:15; compare 1 Sam. 8:7). Pilate caves in, and the execution is ordered. In another unwitting prophecy—much like Caiaphas's when he declared that one man should die for the nation—Pilate arranges for Jesus's execution placard to read: "Jesus of Nazareth, the King of the Jews." The man who asked "what is truth?" a few verses ago has unintentionally proclaimed it clearly. And it's in Aramaic, Latin, and Greek—as though sending a message to the world about the man being crucified.

Before Jesus is crucified, he assigns his mother's care to the beloved disciple. After his death, his body is requested by two secret disciples—Yosef of Arimathea and Naqdimon the Pharisee (Nicodemus). It's a dramatic picture of shifting priorities for these law-abiding Jews; by handling a dead body, they make themselves ritually unclean just moments before Passover. They will have to observe the feast next month on their own under a special provision of the law. They carefully wrap his body according to Jewish customs and lay it in a never-used tomb.

Discuss

- What's the difference between Peter's denial of Jesus and Joseph of Arimathea's secrecy about being a disciple? Why do you think we view one as a monumental failure and the other as an understandable silence?

  _____

  _____

  _____

  _____

- If you had placed all your hopes and reputation on a messiah who ended up dead before he could deliver his people, what would you do next?

  _____

  _____

  _____

  _____

65

A Case Study

Imagine: Looking back, you realize you were just going through a phase. But that phase—that youthful rebellion that mixed you up with all the wrong people—has ruined your life. It opened the door to the reckless act that got you in the horrible position you're in now: awaiting sentencing. And, most likely, a few decades behind bars. What a waste.

So when your attorney comes for an unexpected visit, you're surprised to see her smiling. She tells you to brace yourself for good news: you're being released. You're stunned. You want to ask how . . . why . . . when . . . but you can hardly speak. You know you committed the crime. So what technicality could set you free? It's not a technicality, she says. Someone else—someone you've never even met—is taking the fall.

- Are you more inclined to seek out your savior to thank him or her, to reaffirm your guilt and set the record straight, or to just keep quiet so no one will realize this is a mistake?
- Of those three options, which one—gratitude, guilty conscience, or sweeping it under the rug—best reflects your spiritual attitude toward Jesus? Why?
- How much would you sacrifice for a loved one? A casual friend? A stranger?

Hope Lives

JOHN 20–21

It was supposed to be a new day in Stavronia. A new leadership, a new society, a new hope. And it would have been, if the elections had been allowed to run their course. All the preelection polls indicated a decisive win for the candidate of the future—that is, until the corrupt government's smear campaign finally convinced the populace of a deadly rumor at the last minute, and, just to make sure, an assassin's bullet finally hit its mark. Just like that, the candidate was destined to be a footnote in history, simply the failed leader of a promising movement that lost momentum at the worst possible time. Hope had left the scene.

The government remained in the hands of corrupt men who now had the complete freedom and public backing to stamp out the remains of the movement. The candidate's closest friends knew their odds of survival were slim. They had assumed all along that their allegiance to him would likely have been fatal if he failed. They just didn't expect him to fail. They had underestimated the fickleness of the people, the depravity of the establishment, and the Almighty's reluctance to help. Now their only hope was to hide, to secretly scrounge for basic provisions, until the crisis passed—if, in fact, it ever would.

Losing hope is a traumatic experience that can lead to bitterness, depression, apathy, and emptiness. We turn inward and become isolated, our fears become magnified, and we wonder if we'll ever really "live" again. That was the situation the disciples found themselves in after the dust cleared from the crucifixion. They had placed all their bets on a Galilean miracle-man and witnessed his seizure and execution. Their hopes for ushering

TWO ANGELS

When God gave Moses instructions for making the ark of the covenant, all of the combined details painted a picture of our redemption. One aspect of that picture was the mercy seat: the covering over the ark. Two angels were to be crafted as part of this otherwise flat cover: one at the head, and one at the foot. The angels would face each other with their wings spread upward over the cover. On the day of atonement each year, the high priest would sprinkle sacrificial blood on that cover. The design portrayed two cherubim looking in amazement at the place of extravagant mercy, where blood atones for sins.

When Mary looked into the tomb (20:10–12), she saw a startling picture: a slab of stone and two angels—one at the head, one at the foot. Though the ark had long been lost, the image had remained in Israel's consciousness—and now it was being fulfilled. The sacrifice of Jesus was the kind of mercy that even angels long to see (1 Pet. 1:12).

in a new era in human history vanished literally overnight. In a real sense, when Jesus died, so did they.

Most people find themselves in that situation at least once in life, if not several times. An unexpected death, a betrayal, a sudden turn of events that strips away a dream—the possibilities are many, the results brutally similar. The question we have to ask during those times is whether or not we will believe in the God of the impossible. When circumstances rail against his promises, which will win our hearts? Faith sees through momentary devastation to the ultimate exhilaration of victory. It stays on course and refuses to be moved. And those who hold to faith will see God going to great lengths to restore, refresh, renew, and rebirth the hope that once was lost.

John 20

It's a chaotic scene Sunday morning at the tomb. No one is quite sure what is happening. All they know is that Jesus is gone—and that Mary Magdalene has said she's seen him alive. Some, like John, believe as soon as they see the tomb and/or hear Mary's report. Others aren't so sure. "They still did not understand from Scripture that Jesus had to rise from the dead" (20:12).

Hiding in a locked room—it's only natural that the authorities would want to stamp out the entire movement, not just its leader—the disciples don't know what to do next. Should they look for Jesus? Go back to Galilee and fish? Stay underground until the anti-Jesus fervor dies down? They don't have to decide. Jesus suddenly appears in their midst—he had said he would come to them—and they marvel at the absurdity of fatal wounds on a living body. But this is not a reunion for reminiscing. It's the beginning of the kingdom mission. Jesus is sending his followers out as the Father has sent him. That's a loaded assignment, more than a simple "Now it's your turn." No, Jesus sends his followers out *in the same way* his Father sent him—to "become flesh" and live among those they serve, to love sacrificially, even to pay the ultimate price for their Lord. That's an impossible calling for empty earthen vessels; they'll need to be filled with the breath of life, the wind of the Spirit. So just as God breathed into dust-formed Adam, Jesus breathes on his disciples. The Spirit is on them and in them. They can now forgive others in his name.

But Thomas misses the meeting. Even when his trusted friends tell him what happened, he can't believe. Only if he sees, he says. Jesus obliges, and Thomas falls to his knees. Not only does he honor Jesus as his master, he worships Jesus as his God. And Jesus accepts this; it's true. And the primary purpose of John's book is fulfilled in one climactic statement: "Because you have seen me, you have believed; blessed are those who have not seen and yet have believed" (20:29).

Discuss

- Are you the kind of person who says, "I'll believe it when I see it," or "I'll see it when I believe it"? Why is the latter the normal pattern for faith?

  _____

  _____

  _____

  _____

John 21

It's clear that the disciples don't exactly know what being "sent" should look like yet. Plus, they have to earn a living, as financial

THE BELOVED DISCIPLE

Who is "the disciple Jesus loved" who wrote this testimony of Jesus? Traditionally, he's thought to be John the disciple, the son of Zebedee. That's because John is never mentioned by name in the gospel, which would be odd for someone as close to Jesus as John was; the details in the gospel seem to come from an eye-witness very close to Jesus's ministry; and a second-century bishop (Irenaeus) referred to John as the writer based on the testimony of another bishop who had been "a disciple of John"— presumably, but not necessarily, the apostle.

But there's nothing in the gospel itself that says it was written by John, and a reference to Lazarus as "the one you love" (11:3) has led some to speculate that Lazarus was the disciple who wrote this book. This is possible, since the word "disciple" is very often used in the gospels to refer to followers other than the twelve. Numerous other theories have been developed, including a suggestion that it was written by a follower named John the Elder. But no theory is convincing, and it's entirely possible that the designation of "beloved disciple" comes from a common affectionate expression for the youngest in a family. And John the Apostle was most likely a teenager during much of Jesus's ministry, living nearly until the end of the first century. It is he whom tradition and biblical evidence favors as the one who wrote this remarkable testimony of the light that came into the darkness.

supporters of the Jesus movement have certainly been few and far between since Passover. So some of them return to Galilee and go fishing. And Jesus knows exactly where they are.

He shows up one morning while their boat is still offshore. They've caught nothing all night, but at his word, they cast the nets on the other side of the boat. It's a sign of a new day; fruitfulness is a whole different story after the resurrection. In Peter's enthusiasm, he leaps from the boat and swims to shore, where the Lord has prepared a meal. But is it the Lord? They dare not ask; it has to be. And they enjoy their fellowship together over the harvest the disciples have just reaped.

Then one of the most touching moments in the gospels takes place. Peter still carries the guilt of his three-fold denial of Jesus during that tumultuous night of the arrest. And Jesus, painfully but gently, leads him through a three-fold confession of his love.

What's next? Jesus offers hints of how Peter will follow him in death and the beloved disciple will live a long time. Regardless of how it will go, the command remains the same: "Follow me."

Discuss

- Think of a time when you totally "blew it." In what ways have you seen God restoring you since that time? What wounds from your past might you still need to bring to him?

  _____

  _____

  _____

  _____

- What do you think it would look like in your life to be sent out in the same way the Father sent the Son? What steps do you need to take to live out that mission?

  _____

  _____

  _____

  _____

A CASE STUDY

Imagine: For three years, you've undergone rigorous, comprehensive training—you and your fellow trainees consider yourselves the Navy Seals of the Spirit. Your course has involved physical, mental, and emotional endurance; sharpening "sixth" senses of discernment and spiritual hearing; hours and even days of fasting and prayer; withstanding ridicule; and learning to access supernatural power. These skills haven't come easy. In fact, you're still light-years behind your teacher. Even so, he says you're ready. Now's the time. He's sending you out to do what you've been trained for—spread his kingdom through wisdom, power, and love against all manner of opposition and at all costs.

- Would this kind of situation make you nervous, or would you be eager to get started? What fears or reservations might you have?
- To what degree do you currently view your discipleship in these terms? How might this sense of mission fit into your current life situation?
- Does this picture of discipleship change how you think about following Jesus? If so, how?

Conclusion

The re-genesis has begun, and the members of the new creation have a mission: to go into the world as he was sent into the world. That means being light in darkness, breathing his Spirit into the environment around us, doing the kinds of works he did at a greater level (14:12), and enduring the opposition that inevitably comes. In a real sense, his people are also to be the Word that comes in the flesh. It isn't an easy mission, but no other mission in life is satisfying. As you live your days, watch and see what he does in you, through you, and around you. The new creation is springing up everywhere.

Leader's Notes

Session 1

John 3. When discussing how participants have experienced the "wind" of the Spirit, you may encounter a wide variety of responses, including some that indicate unfamiliarity with the idea of being blown by the Spirit. This can lead to a very fruitful discussion, but don't feel obliged to have the group resolve all questions or define exactly what being led by the Spirit means. By nature and God's design, this issue defies precision. Some degree of mystery is expected and even necessary.

Session 2

A Case Study. The point of this discussion is, of course, to highlight some of the dynamics people wrestled with when they encountered Jesus. He didn't fit their expectations or their interpretation of Scripture, and was declared a false teacher by most well-respected theologians. Encourage participants to try to determine which segment of the crowd/followers/disciples they would have fit into if they had been on the scene in John 6.

Session 3

John 7. When discussing the question of how the religious leaders' lives would change if they believed Jesus, consider several different aspects of their lives. Internally, they would have received God's peace, of course. But what would have happened to them externally in terms of their career? Social status and influence? Religious practices?

Session 4

A Case Study. This conversation could go in several different directions. The sample prayer may reflect the actual prayer of one of your group's participants very accurately. Be sensitive to that possibility, but do emphasize the positive answers to the last question: "In what ways might God use this situation for his glory?" He really may have a specific time in mind for a dramatic answer, which would certainly glorify him. But the comfort he gives, the bonds of dependence he strengthens in us, the power that shows up in our weakness . . . all of these are also manifestations of his glory. Help your group discuss some ways to make their prayers centered on the glory of God more than on the needs of the pray-er—affirming, of course, that God is deeply concerned for both.

Session 5

John 12. When discussing the questions about 12:24–25, it may be helpful to compare these verses with Matthew 16:24–25, where the same thoughts are expressed, but in slightly different terms. The differences will help highlight the meaning of Jesus's words about "loving" and "hating" our life.

Session 6

John 13. The discussion of how to practically "wash people's feet" provides a great opportunity for your group to take some action. Consider committing to a service project or a practical initiative to do together.

Session 7

John 17. When discussing the personal application of this high priestly prayer, encourage participants to try this exercise later: substitute their name for all the "they" pronouns, especially in verses 20–26. This will help bring home the point that Jesus's prayer was prayed for all of his people throughout history—including each person reading it.

John 18. In your group, there are probably some people who are completely open about their relationship with the Lord and others who are very reluctant to discuss their faith with non-Christians. Explore the reactions participants get (or fear getting) when they are vocal about faith issues.

Session 8

A Case Study. If there's time, broaden your discussion of discipleship to cover how your culture interprets "following Jesus." What opposition do disciples have to face in society? How do they compare/contrast to the twelve disciples? What kinds of endurance, mental toughness, and preparation are required to follow Jesus fully today?

Bibliography

Arnold, Clinton E. *Zondervan Illustrated Bible Backgrounds Commentary*. Grand Rapids: Zondervan, 2002.

Bock, Darrell L. *Jesus according to Scripture: Restoring the Portrait from the Gospels*. Grand Rapids: Baker Academic, 2006.

Chilton, Bruce, et al. *The Cambridge Companion to the Bible*. Cambridge and New York: Cambridge University Press, 1997.

Geisler, Norman L. *A Popular Survey of the New Testament*. Grand Rapids: Baker Academic, 2007.

Kaiser, Walter C., Jr., and Duane Garrett. *Archaeological Study Bible*. Grand Rapids: Zondervan, 2006.

Keener, Craig S. *The IVP Bible Background Commentary: New Testament*. Downers Grove, IL: InterVarsity Press, 1993.

McQuaid, Elwood. *The Outpouring: Jesus in the Feasts of Israel*. Bellmawr, NJ: Friends of Israel Gospel Ministry, Inc., 1990.

Ryken, Leland, and Philip Graham Ryken, eds. *The Literary Study Bible*. Wheaton, IL: Crossway, 2007.

Stern, David H. *Jewish New Testament Commentary*. Clarksville, MD: Jewish New Testament Publications, Inc., 1992.

**WALK
THRU THE
BIBLE®**

Helping people everywhere
live God's Word

For more than three decades, Walk Thru the Bible has created discipleship materials and cultivated leadership networks that together are reaching millions of people through live seminars, print publications, audiovisual curricula, and the Internet. Known for innovative methods and high-quality resources, we serve the whole body of Christ across denominational, cultural, and national lines. Through our strong and cooperative international partnerships, we are strategically positioned to address the church's greatest need: developing mature, committed, and spiritually reproducing believers.

Walk Thru the Bible communicates the truths of God's Word in a way that makes the Bible readily accessible to anyone. We are committed to developing user-friendly resources that are Bible centered, of excellent quality, life changing for individuals, and catalytic for churches, ministries, and movements; and we are committed to maintaining our global reach through strategic partnerships while adhering to the highest levels of integrity in all we do.

Walk Thru the Bible partners with the local church worldwide to fulfill its mission, helping people "walk thru" the Bible with greater clarity and understanding. Live seminars and small group curricula are taught in over 45 languages by more than 80,000 people in more than 70 countries, and more than 100 million devotionals have been packaged into daily magazines, books, and other publications that reach over five million people each year.

Walk Thru the Bible
4201 North Peachtree Road
Atlanta, GA 30341-1207
770-458-9300
www.walkthru.org

Read the entire Bible in one year, thanks to the systematic reading plan in the best-selling **Daily Walk** devotional.

The **Daily Walk** devotional magazine includes book introductions, charts outlining book and chapter themes, and background information on each day's reading. Insightful observations shed light on the culture, the history, and the context of passages. Each daily reading is loaded with helpful applications that enable you to apply biblical truth to your life. Readers are sure to find the time they spend in the Bible more productive and rewarding than ever before.

Ideal for church-wide or group Bible study, bulk subscriptions to **Daily Walk** offering significant savings can be purchased online at www.walkthru.org. Discounted individual subscriptions are also available online.

WALK THRU THE BIBLE

www.walkthru.org

Individual Orders: 800-877-5539   Bulk Orders: 800-998-0814